Quilt it & colour it

or the art of doodling in fabric

Rosemary Muntus

Three things you love to do

1 Doodling

2 Quilting

3 Colouring

When you were young you probably loved doodling and colouring-in. As you grew older you got hooked on quilting. So here's some very good news – this technique combines all three! And, for a little extra fun, it turns your ideas about quilting back to front. Because the quilting comes before the colouring...

Just at the moment doodling and colouring-in are all the rage. They aid concentration, promote inner peace and add beauty and interest to our lives. The techniques outlined here do all of these things. (And you happen to find quilting a bit stressful, then the doodling and colouring will soon calm you down...)

How to doodle

So let's start with doodling. If you're feeling inspired you can doodle straight on to cloth with your sewing machine. If you find drawing difficult, you may find the sewing machine liberating.

But I recommend that you also have a small notebook to hand with a pencil and pen, and use it to play and to jot down ideas. I started on the cloth and then went back to the drawing board, as it were. Now I use both. We will explore ideas and techniques for doodling so as to improve the quilting skills themselves. Doing a little every day or even once a week makes a real difference.

Analysing your doodles can be helpful, and you can build up a whole repertoire of useful fills and patterns. These can be abstract or more pictorial, but you want to create shapes that you can fill with colour and possibly with shading.

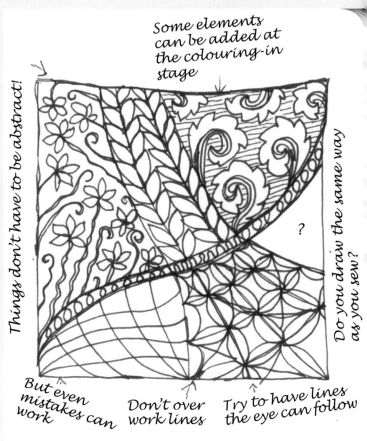

Some elements can be added at the colouring-in stage

Things don't have to be abstract!

Do you draw the same way as you sew?

But even mistakes can work

Don't over work lines

Try to have lines the eye can follow

Think just how you would quilt this? Where you would have to travel stitch to get to new areas? How do your stitches divide up an area?

A page from my own doodling book, with some extra thoughts and ideas jotted down.

On paper, try to create areas of contrast and interest which can then be coloured in.

Imagine yourself quilting these shapes as you draw them - aim for continuous lines.

Optional exercise - creating a tangle

The next two pages give a brief introduction to Zentangling® and show how you convert a tangle into a fully worked piece.

This exercise is based on Zentangling®, but think how your design could be stitched on a larger scale.

Exercise

1 Photocopy or draw the square on good paper.

2 Join up the dots with a fine or medium black marker pen to make your tile.

3 Divide the tile into at least five different areas

4 Fill each area with a different quiltable pattern.

You can buy cards, but you can also download and print out these and larger templates from my website - www.muntus.com.

Tangles are usually worked on good quality paper or card and are usually 4" or 10cm square with a bit of clear space around them.

Have you tried Zentangling®?

If you feel a bit unsure about doodling your quilt patterns onto a clean piece of paper or cloth, you may find the rules that Zentangling® imposes helpful.

Don't get too involved or you may never get round to sewing. But - like quilting - zentangling gets easier if you practice a little. Just doing one tangle every day will help you make great leaps forward.

You create tiles which are approximately 4" or 10cm square. Draw a frame freehand and divide the square into a variety of areas with more or less wiggly lines (known as 'strings'). Fill these areas with different Tangles. There are as many of these as there are quilting patterns, and you will find lovely books out there which show in simple steps how to draw a Tangle. Many of them are featured on Pinterest and on any number of individual Zentanglers' websites.

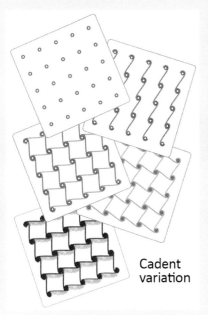

Cadent variation

Here are the steps used to create a variant of an original Tangle by one of the inventors of Zentangling®, Maria Thomas.

In full Tangle creation you create both the pattern and any fills and shading. Working through the tangle helps to sort out where to quilt so as to minimise the number of stops and starts needed. Not all tangles make good quilt designs.

As always, some designs work better than others, and you will quickly develop favourites. It works both ways, too: you will probably start

A few of my own attempts at creatir Zentangle® tile

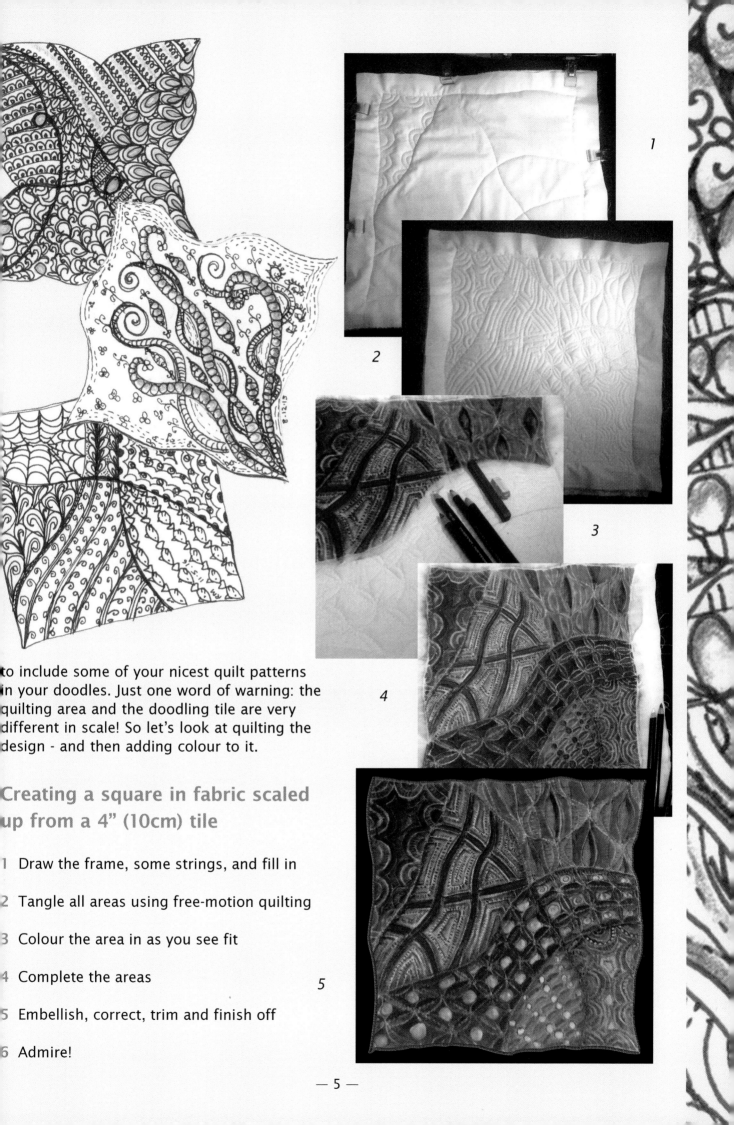

to include some of your nicest quilt patterns
in your doodles. Just one word of warning: the
quilting area and the doodling tile are very
different in scale! So let's look at quilting the
design - and then adding colour to it.

Creating a square in fabric scaled up from a 4" (10cm) tile

1 Draw the frame, some strings, and fill in

2 Tangle all areas using free-motion quilting

3 Colour the area in as you see fit

4 Complete the areas

5 Embellish, correct, trim and finish off

6 Admire!

Machine quilting

More and more people are experimenting with machine quilting. You may even have access to a long-arm quilting machine, the ultimate tool for this technique.

A domestic machine works perfectly well, though: all my pieces were done on one of my trusty Pfaffs. We will look at all the things that can help you doodle-quilt on cloth, and what to do when things go wrong (or even if you run out of ideas). Again, little and often will really help you to advance. Even small pieces can become masterpieces (or at least useful learning tools)

Using textiles, you can doodle in the same way. Create enclosed areas of contrast and interest to colour in.

Create a fabric doodle 16" × 16" (40cm)

Be brave and try quilting directly onto the cloth. It does work, and it is sometimes easier than trying to slavishly recreate a pre-drawn pattern. You need some sort of framework to anchor the layers together. Sketching in this isn't cheating.

1 Cut two pieces of cotton 22" × 22" (55cm) and cut one or two layers of wadding approximately the same size.

2 Using a ruler, mark your working area by ruling approximately 3" (7.5cm) in from all the edges. Marking is easiest on a firm surface but can be done even after the quilt sandwich is assembled.

3 Sketch in any long dividing lines you wish to apply to your project. This will make more sense after you have experimented a bit with freehand quilting techniques. Use a grey or silver pencil, or one that will match your final colour scheme.

4 (Optional) You can mark out a formal design before assembling your layers. If you are using white cloth you should be able to trace your design – the new LED light-boxes make this very easy.

5 Pin or clip the layers together and with the sewing machine set up either for free embroidery or normal sewing, stitch a first line across the sewing area.

Both doodling and colouring-in are supposed to be calming activities. Try to keep calm and let your hands guide you in pattern making. The trick with free quilting is to get your hands and your speed control (usually foot operated) in synchronisation with one another. So when you move slowly, you sew slowly; speed up, and you need to increase the

The cotton batting sandwich with the border and some dividing lines lightly pencilled in.

foot pressure. If you fail to do this you will get rather large stitches - which isn't a total tragedy as you can always sew over this line of stitching again.

6 Sew the main dividing lines first either as single lines or as braided rows of stitching (See McTavishing on the next page).

7 Backtrack by sewing over existing lines as much as possible to build up and secure the working area.

The basic outline of the quilting for the wall hanging shown on page 9. Be as bold as you can and if you create an area of particular interest or beauty, try to repeat that somewhere else.

Quilt doodling a white square (coloured thread was used to make the quilting more visible)

8 Fill in the areas in between this with patterns you like, or find easy to do.

9 Try to create areas that can be coloured in easily. You need closed shapes.

Things you need for quilting

- **Quiltable fabric.** White cotton. I use PFD (prepared for dyeing) cotton available from many sources but I also like Kona Cotton and Calico.

- **Batting.** I usually use Cotton classic but wool is fantastic.

- **Marking pen or pencil.** I mainly use a silver or pale grey one to draw in the bare bones of the design and the approximate outer limit of the quilting area.

- **Ruler to mark straight lines.** Quilters' ruler helps keep everything square. (And 5cm is equivalent to 2" for most folk)

- **Optionally a lightbox...** The new LED ones are fairly cheap and easy to use.

- **Quilting thread.** Leah Day recommends Isacord as it is very tough. I generally use white for both the bobbin and top thread.

- **Small scissors** and an unpicker which you shouldn't really need.

- **Sewing machine** set up for free embroidery

- **Optional quilting paraphernalia** such as spring foot, quilter's gloves, Teflon sheet. I really like the first of these but the gloves and the sheet really come into their own when doing bigger projects.

Quilting 1 – the McTavishing approach

Karen McTavish is a long-arm quilter in the States who has given her name to a simple flowing quilting technique which can be done very effectively on a domestic sewing machine.

With or without a pencil guide, start by sewing a long wiggly line across your work area.

1 Add additional lines to the piece, echoing the first line but starting and finishing at the same point.

2 Now travel along one of these lines and branch off at a suitable point (or where you put a guide line in). Remember this is meant to be a meditative and calming activity.

3 Echo this line several times and then either branch off from this or travel back to first set of lines.

4 Try to divide your work area into five or six interesting areas. The echoing lines of stitching can be close together or they can be more widely spread apart they can even cross one another. Do however try to make completely enclosed areas.

You needn't sew freehand: just 'wobble' ordinary lines of stitching. Even so, some variations are much easier using freehand techniques, especially as you learn to sew smoothly backwards or forwards or from side to side. And even with a walking foot it is easier to avoid the quilting bubbling up the cloth. But if you smooth everything as you go, it can be done.

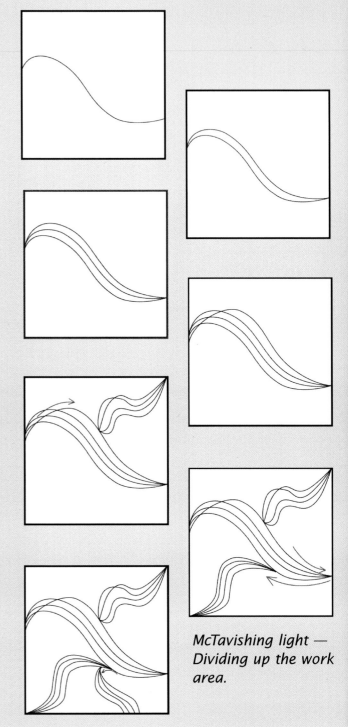

McTavishing light — Dividing up the work area.

These first diagrams are 'McTavishing light': they aren't as curvy as they would be in the original technique, where great folds and spirals form the basic skeleton. We need to stabilise the work, and these first rows of stitching do just that.

You can also divide your area with single rows of stitches, very similar to the strings found in classic Zentangling® (see page 4).

If you want to McTavish in the style of the mistress of the technique, you can now add additional lines and curly bits and then fill in the spaces in between using a simple arcing technique, or one of the other fairly simple fills she recommends.

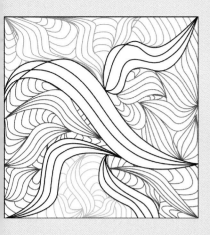

McTavishing with additional arcs.

Or with two or more of your own favourite fills.

Quilting 2 – fancy doodling

I am building up a list of quilters who make interesting fill patterns for machine quilting. The first is Leah Day, who initially created 365 fill patterns but still has the occasional need to create new ones. And if you doodle on paper you too will start to create patterns that you will want to quilt.

The best advice I can give is to quilt a bit every day and try out patterns on a piece of spare wadded fabric. It takes time to get truly proficient but even your try-outs may grow into exciting pieces. You can always backtrack and resew bits. Alternatively just let yourself go, and fill the different areas with a whole range of different patterns.

If you want the full doodling experience you should now have several areas where you can develop your doodles. There are two ways of doing this.

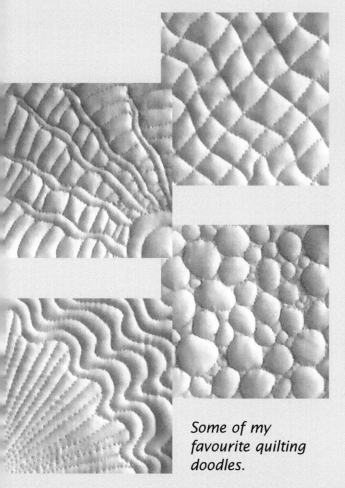

Some of my favourite quilting doodles.

Wall-hanging, Egyptian 3, *39cm × 39cm with some of my favourite patterns.*

1 Draw designs out to fill the gaps using a pale pencil and then sew these designs

2 Sew the designs directly onto the fabric, designing fills as you go.

This second method may seem more difficult, but it is actually rather easier and I find it less demanding than trying to follow and stitch drawn lines accurately.

Build a repertoire of designs you like. Many of Leah Day's designs are suitable, but go for one which gives you closed shapes that can easily be coloured in, and which creates boundaries that can easily be abutted against other designs.

There are lots of books and on-line resources for doodling and for the more specific zen doodling, as well as lovely colouring-in books.

Many quilting experts advise you to try drawing or doodling the designs you want to sew. In this way you will develop a 'quilt memory' which will make the actual sewing easier.

In the next section we will look at how you can colour the pieces in. But here are some ideas to help you with your quilt doodling – and an optional exercise to create a colouring space without the need to do any free machine quilting.

Zendoodle 2, 30cm × 30cm. I have done this tile 3 times so I can confirm copying existing patterns is tricky.

Zendoodle 3, 30cm × 30cm. Fortunately they are all designs that are easy to do.

Things that will help you create fills

1 Look at some of the new colouring books made for adults

2 Study quilts especially those that show machine fill designs

3 Study further the Zentangling® phenomenon. There are some great books on this.

4 Have the right pens, pencils, papers at hand to doodle.

5 Save your own scribbles and doodles

6 Build up a collection of favourite designs, and practice them both as doodles and as fills

Things that will help you quilt

1   When sewing, try to be as relaxed as possible about the quilting.

2   Deal with one area at a time and envisage a pattern that will look good in that shape. Flow into the area, sewing slowly, and put in any major structures that appeal. These could be nice curly hook shapes or they could be petal shapes or wiggly lines.

3   Try to keep the stitching lines continuous, but don't be afraid of sewing back along a line or even re-sewing the line the way you want it rather than the way it came out.

4   Only very rarely does a line look so ugly or out of place that you need to unpick it.

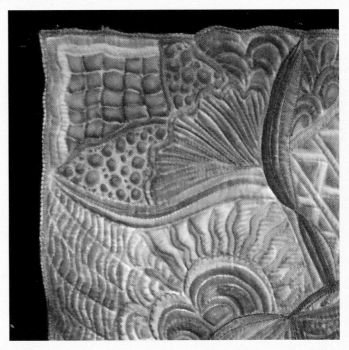

Just more doodles (detail). Wall-hanging, Egyptian 2, 49cm × 49cm.

5   Ideally I sew with white thread in needle and bobbin, but to make it easier to see what's happening try a darker upper thread.

Still want the white on white effect? If you've sorted out the tension problems first you can flip the finished work over and use the underside as your canvas.

You will need to be scrupulous about finishing your loose ends off or you will have fun and games trimming away sewn-in loose ends. I have been there myself, and trimmed away a lot of unwanted threads.

A slightly earlier piece. Wall-hanging, Mac-Zangle 2, 39cm × 39cm.

6   Fill spaces in the areas with appropriate doodles, arcs or lines. Try to keep creating closed spaces that can be individually coloured.

Colouring-in without free quilting

I really got excited about colouring my fabric after I had been playing with free machine quilting doodles, but I had used them before to enliven my experiments using an attachment to help you sew circles.

So if you want to get colouring and you are still just practicing your free machine doodling you might like the exercise that follows...

For this doodle I only used the various embroidery stitches on my machine for the quilting.

My first attempt at using Inktense pencils. Circles of embroidery stitches sewn on calico. Coloured-in dry, and wetted and iron set afterwards.

Make a machine-quilted mug-rug

1 Cut out a piece of white cotton 14" × 10" (35cm × 25cm), a backing the same size and one or two pieces of wadding ideally heat resistant. Pin or clip together. (The backing can be any colour but white is fine)

2 Assemble your wadding sandwich, and clamp or pin it securely.

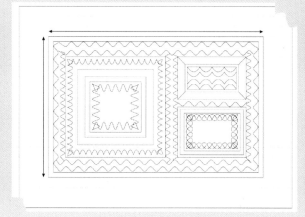

3 Mark a border 1½" (4cm) in from the edges and machine stitch this all the way round.

4 Sew another row of straight stitching ¼" (1cm) inside this.

5 Using the fancy stitches as well as straight stitching divide the area up in to the cup space and the cookie space. Use the side of your foot to keep rows straight.

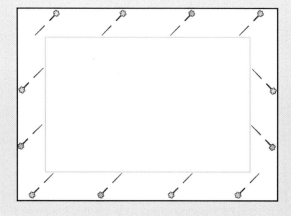

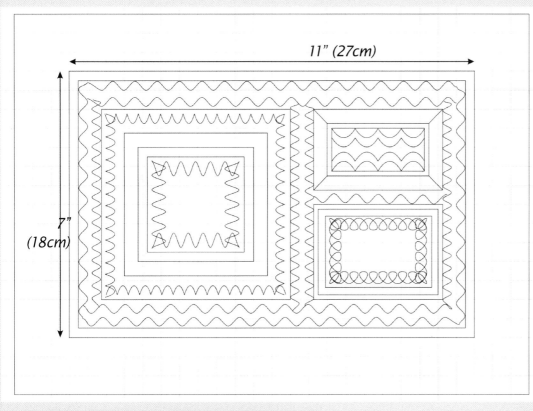

11" (27cm)

7" (18cm)

Basic plan of the mug-rug. Use the stitches found on your own sewing machine.

Aim to create closed areas that can be coloured in.

A full sized .pdf file is available to download on my website.

6 Colour in the area when quilted (see p14) using either method or a combination. Use the colours of a favourite mug if you need a colour scheme

Work from the outer edges towards the centre, aiming to produce individual spaces to colour in.

7 Trim close to the outer line of sewing and then finish off using either of the methods shown on page 20.

Colouring the cloth dry

This method lets you colour in very precisely. You apply the colour first and then paint on textile medium or aloe vera

1 Quilt your 'canvas' either using white thread above and below, or a thread colour that will be an asset to the design.

Alternatively thread a colour you can see on the top while quilting and white below and turn the quilting over to colour the reverse side. Remember to trim all threads away as you go as the underside needs to be as 'clean' as the side you quilted from.

2 Using pencils or blocks work colour into each area and then paint on textile medium using suitably sized brushes. Habicht puts out only a small blob of the textile medium at a time as it quickly becomes sticky and dries up.

Paint carefully each coloured shape with the medium and while the fabric is still wet add additional colour or texture to your shapes.

3 Alternatively you can paint diluted fabric medium over the whole area if you are happy to have a little bleeding.

4 Allow the medium to dry and steam iron, using a protective cloth to set the colour.

I have used Leah Day's machine embroidery pattern so as to compare the results more easily.

Using Derwent Inktense pencils and then applying textile medium as I go.

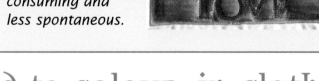

The colours stay crisp, but the cloth is stiffer and the process is more time consuming and less spontaneous.

Things you will need to colour-in cloth

- Suitable colouring media. I use Lakeland Inktense Pencils and Blocks as well as other fabric colouring media. Sharpies or other permanent markers can be used to embellish. I particularly like metallic ones. Textile medium and textile paints

- Brushes, both thick and thin

- Sponges and shapers or bits of rag to dampen cloth

- Aloe Vera gel as a aid to stop colours running

- Ironing clothes to protect both iron and ironing board

- A steam iron and board.

Dampening the cloth before painting

How easily colour is added depends on how wet your 'canvas' is. There will be some bleeding when the colour flows into adjacent areas. This can be made to work for you, or minimised by using water sparingly, letting it dry slightly or adding a barrier to minimise the bleed.

This is how I started. It is a bit more risky because you will get the colours bleeding into one another. However it is more sensual, you can make good use of the quilted 'texture' and you can mix colours easily.

The pink colours have run or bled, making the whole block rather pink.

1 Prepare your quilt as above.

2 Using water or diluted textile medium, dampen individual areas using a small paint brush. For larger areas use a flat paint brush or a sponge squeegee.

3 Use blocks to colour large areas.

4 Use the pencils to create additional detail and depth.

5 Iron dry, using a protective piece of white cotton to soak up any excess colour.

6 You can make the bleed work for you.

7 Experiment with mixing and matching colours.

8 Trim and finish off as required.

You can add colour and shading very easily. Use an iron, with an ironing cloth, to dry your work. Add extra colour as required.

For pale colours apply colour very lightly and try to spread the colour quickly with the paint brush. You can also make a paste of the colour blocks and paint the colour on directly, or correct your work using a white pencil or a white block of Derwent Inktense.

Preventing bleed with Aloe Vera

Aloe Vera, a clear gel with several beauty and therapeutic uses, can be a great ally when colouring in your designs with Inktense pens and blocks. You can paint selected areas with it in the same way that you would use a textile medium. You can also use it on areas you have already painted, where it will provide an effective barrier.

The blues and the greens in this ship picture were applied to a wetted design, and I encouraged further bleed using a wetted paintbrush. After drying it I blocked out the blue areas with aloe vera, then applied the yellow and red colours by dampening the fabric again with a small paint brush and using Inktense pencils.

Making bleed work for you while protecting some colours using Aloe Vera. The base design is 'Lost at Sea' UT6928 from Urban Threads.

Working with machine embroideries

Doodling is great fun, but you can also colour in other people's designs. After I started to learn free machine quilting with Leah Day she brought out embroidery files for some of her favourite free machine quilting patterns.

The two runners on pages 18 and 19 are based on her 'Reflections of Nature' embroidery designs. The samples on pages 15 and 16 use her 'Stitch 'n paint Love' design.

The ship design above, and the bag on the right, were both produced by Urban Threads. There are many ready-made designs like these that you can use, and I have enjoyed the many opportunities they have given for playing with colour.

Urban Threads produce many lovely designs. In Spring 2016 they produced this one as a competition piece. The challenge was to colour it in, and the prize was embroidery thread. I didn't finish my bag in time but the design works well and I enjoyed colouring it in! This is 'Craft is Art' – UT13537.

If you have an embroidery machine, please do try them out. Look for designs that have light stitching, that are single colour designs (Redwork and Bluework) and might even be labelled 'Doodle designs'.

Working with less abstract designs

I have themes I always come back to. One is a view through an arch, a window, or vegetation - like this one.

This piece started out as a doodle in my notebook. Then I pencilled in the outlines so I would know where the main elements were when I started sewing.

You can still let the quilting line take you where it wants to, but this way you will start out with a basic structure.

Above: Wall hanging Tropical View, *45" × 21½" (115cm × 80cm). Cotton with woollen batting and polyester quilting thread. Inktense blocks used, especially white for the clouds.*

Right: My original drawing, which is only about 4" × 3" (10cm × 7.5cm).

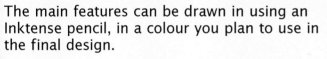

Left and below: Fishy McFishFace, *a small panel before and after colouring in. Finished off using the cord and zig-zag method (page 20).*

The main features can be drawn in using an Inktense pencil, in a colour you plan to use in the final design.

Now you can quilt your design and add all sorts of ideas and doodles to make your piece simply zing!

Finally you can add or emphasise details as you colour in your work.

Gallery and further ideas

A Beach Tangle *45"× 45" (115cm × 115cm)*
A wall hanging made in cotton, painted with
bead embellishments and finished off with
conventional strip binding.

Table runner 1, *10½"× 34½" (26cm × 87cm).*
Four of Leah Day's fills machine embroidered
and coloured in. Finished off with chenille.

Table
runner 2,
detail.

Flowers on silk, *15"× 15" (38cm × 38cm) a*
hanging or cushion cover piece with narrow
border. Silk doesn't always take colour as easily
but can have lovely textures. Not quilted as
intensively as some other pieces and using
bleed to colour the unquilted areas.

Life on the Reef *32½" × 45" (115cm × 80cm). Wall hanging finished off with a painted border and chenille thread.*

Mac-Zangle 2, *15¼" × 15¼" (39cm × 39cm) One of my first pieces, and finished off using zig-zagging and rat's tail.*

Table runner 2, *10" × 49" (25cm × 125cm). Six of Leah Day's fills, machine embroidered and coloured in. Machine stitched border, finished off by taking the front to the back and hemming in place.*

Finishing off

Items can be finished off conventionally with a binding strip (See *Beach Tangle* on page 18) but they can also be finished off using machine stitching with or without a cord or length of fancy thread to give the edge definition.

1 Trim your piece neatly,

2 Zig-zag round the outer edge to hold the layers firmly together. Trim away any loose threads. Use medium width and an open zig-zag. Take care with the corners.

3 Take wool or stranded cotton, rat's tail or bouclé in a matching or contrasting colour and starting away from a corner set up your sewing machine with a wider, tighter zig-zag and catch your thick tread onto the edge. Use a suitable tool (here the end of a stitch unpicker) or your finger to ensure that the thread stays tight.

4 Trim the thread where you started and then as you come round to the start point taper the thread as you trim it and catch it with a few extra stitches.

5 Add additional decorative stitches as required.

Another method involves trimming the backing and the wadding tightly to the edge of the work.

1 Using a rotary cutter trim the piece of work with at least ¾" (2cm) outside the quilted area.

2 Pin the top layer back on itself and trim away the wadding and backing tightly along the edge of your work.

3 Unpin the top fabric, take to the back and hem in place carefully mitring your corners.